Earth and Heaven

An Anthology of Myth Poetry

Recent Poetry Published by Fitzhenry & Whiteside

RINGING HERE & THERE: A NATURE CALENDAR	Brian Bartlett
ALONGSIDE	Anne Compton
A RELIQUARY AND OTHER POEMS	Daryl Hine
DIGRESSIONS: PROSE POEMS, COLLAGE POEMS AND SKETCHES	Robyn Sarah
WHITE SHEETS	Beverley Bie Brahic
ASKING QUESTIONS INDOORS AND OUT	Anne Compton
&: A SERIAL POEM	Daryl Hine
SKY ATLAS	Alan R. Wilson
THE DAY IN MOSS	Eric Miller
RECOLLECTED POEMS: 1951-2004	Daryl Hine
CROWN AND RIBS	Blaise Moritz
THE HERMIT'S KISS	Richard Teleky
MAPS OF INVARIANCE	John Smith
PROCESSIONAL	Anne Compton
INSECTS	Iain Deans

Earth and Heaven

AN ANTHOLOGY OF MYTH POETRY

Edited by
Amanda Jernigan
AND
Evan Jones

Fitzhenry & Whiteside

Copyright © 2015 Amanda Jernigan, Evan Jones

All rights reserved. No part of this publication may be reproduced, stored in a retrieval system or transmitted, in any form or by any means, without the prior written permission of Fitzhenry & Whiteside or, in case of photocopying or other reprographic copying, a licence from Access Copyright (Canadian Copyright Licensing Agency) 1 Yonge Street, Suite 1900, Toronto, ON, M5E 1E5, Fax (416) 868-1621.

Published in Canada by Fitzhenry & Whiteside,
195 Allstate Parkway, Markham, ON, L3R 4T8
Published in the United States by Fitzhenry & Whiteside, 311 Washington Street, Brighton, Massachusetts, 02135

www.fitzhenry.ca godwit@fitzhenry.ca

We acknowledge with thanks the Canada Council for the Arts and the Ontario Arts Council for their support of our publishing program. We acknowledge the financial support of the Government of Canada through the Canada Book Fund (CBF) for our publishing activities.

 Canada Council for the Arts Conseil des Arts du Canada  ONTARIO ARTS COUNCIL CONSEIL DES ARTS DE L'ONTARIO

Library and Archives Canada Cataloguing in Publication
Earth and heaven : an anthology of myth poetry / edited by Amanda Jernigan and Evan Jones.
ISBN 978-1-55455-376-1 (pbk.)
1. Canadian poetry (English). 2. Myth--Poetry. 3. Myth in literature.
I. Jernigan, Amanda, 1978-, editor II. Jones, Evan, 1973-, editor
PS8287.M9E27 2015   C811'.608037   C2015-902164-2

Publisher Cataloging-in-Publication Data (U.S.)
Earth and heaven : an anthology of myth poetry / edited by Amanda Jernigan and Evan Jones.
[124] pages : cm.
Summary: "Jernigan and Jones celebrate the vitality and diversity of poetry inspired by, or in conversation with, myth. Looking back to the early 20th century and forward to the contemporary, *Earth and Heaven* gathers voices and stories as it moves through 'four ages' of mythic history." – from the publisher.
ISBN: 978-1-55455-376-1 (pbk.)
1. Canadian poetry—20th century. I. Jernigan, Amanda. II. Jones, Evan. III. Title.
811.5408 dc23   PR9195.7.E3684 2015

Design by Daniel Choi.
Cover image reprinted from *Out of the Wood* by Rosemary Kilbourn by permission of the Porcupine's Quill.
Copyright © Rosemary Kilbourn, 2012.

Printed and bound in Canada.

i.m. Daryl Hine, Jay Macpherson, and Richard Outram,

and

for our children

CONTENTS

Amanda Jernigan	*Preface: The Last Mythopoet*	9
Evan Jones	*Earth and Heaven: An Introduction*	23
Jay Macpherson	*The Marriage of Earth and Heaven*	29

I. IN THE BEGINNING

Harry Thurston	*[Unknown]*	33
Daniel David Moses	*Crow Out Early*	34
Douglas LePan	*River-God*	35
Gwendolyn MacEwen	*Our Child Which Art in Heaven*	36
Margaret Avison	*Birth Day*	37
Souvankham Thammavongsa	*The Bible, Notes On*	39
George Johnston	*Creation*	40
John Terpstra	*Genesis*	42
Beverley Bie Brahic	*PS: Book of Eve*	43
Anne Compton	*Birdlore*	44

II. LOVES OF THE GODS AND METAMORPHOSES

Robert Bringhurst	*[from Ursa Major]*	49
Darren Bifford	*Wedding in Fire Country*	51
Leonard Cohen	*Song*	54
Alfred Bailey	*Gluskap's Daughter*	55
Diana Brebner	*Frozen*	57
Mary Dalton	*Salt Mounds, St. John's Harbour*	59
Steven Heighton	*Were You to Die*	60
Sue Sinclair	*Orpheus Meets Eurydice in the Underworld*	62
Robert Gibbs	*Depth of Field*	64
Bruce Taylor	*Orphée*	65
Peter Sanger	*After Monteverdi*	67
Mark Callanan	*The Myth of Orpheus*	68

III. THE HEROES

Elise Partridge	*Sisyphus: The Sequel*	73
Daryl Hine	*Patroclus Putting on the Armour of Achilles*	75
Don McKay	*Fates Worse Than Death*	76
Jeffery Donaldson	*Troy*	78
Marius Kociejowski	*Coast*	79
Ricardo Sternberg	[from *Map of Dreams*]	82
Michael Crummey	*Odysseus as a Boy*	84
Richard Greene	*St. Ignace*	85
Carmine Starnino	*Deaths of the Saints*	87
Wayne Clifford	*Jane Relents*	88
Brian Bartlett	*A Skater Tale*	89
James Reaney	*Don Quixot de la Verismo*	91
Norm Sibum	*Embarkation of the Argonauts*	93
M. Travis Lane	*Gold Fleece*	94

IV. THE PASSING AND AFTERLIFE OF THE GODS

P.K. Page	*The Gold Sun*	97
E.J. Pratt	*Myth and Fact*	99
W.W.E. Ross	*Delphic Apollo*	101
Kerry-Lee Powell	*The Answers*	102
Warren Heiti	*Sonnets to Orpheus 1.3*	104
Anne Wilkinson	*Twilight of the Gods*	105
Robyn Sarah	*A Confused Heart*	106
A.F. Moritz	*To the Still Unborn*	108
Eric Ormsby	*Jaham's Poetic Manifesto*	109
John Thompson	*[Ghazal XXI]*	110
James Pollock	*Sailing to Babylon*	111
Richard Outram	*Ms Cassie Abandoned*	112
Jay Macpherson	*The Love-Song of Jenny Lear*	113

SOME NOTES ON CONTEXT   115
ACKNOWLEDGEMENTS   121

Amanda Jernigan
Preface : The Last Mythopoet

>   Hear the voice of the Bard!
>   Want to know where I've been?
>   Under the frost-hard
>   Ground with Hell's Queen,
>   Whom there I embraced
>   In the dark as she lay,
>   With worms defaced,
>   Her lips gnawed away
>   – What's that? Well, maybe
>   Not everybody's dame,
>   But a sharp baby
>   All the same.

This is "The Rymer," by Jay Macpherson (1931-2012), rymer; queen of the mid-century, Toronto-based myth poets; and to some extent the presiding spirit of this collection. It's a poem that suggests that *all* poets (or at least all Poets) are myth poets: their haunts otherworldly; their companions, too.

Not everyone would agree. There are critics for whom myth poetry is, if anything, a *was:* a short-lived literary movement that grew up here in Canada under the influence of the mythopoeic criticism of Northrop Frye, and died out when its chief practitioners – Macpherson and James Reaney (1926-2008) are the two most often cited – went on to other things. In the May/June 2013 issue of *PN Review,* Evan Jones called me, only half-jokingly, "the last mythopoet": "the only heir to a tradition that was once central and has now died out." Romantic as it was to be considered a rarity – a last unicorn, a Lonesome George – I felt in my gut that Jones was wrong. For myth poetry – the kind of poetry that not only uses myth but makes and remakes it – seemed to me alive and well in the work of my contemporaries.

I told Jones as much when we spoke on the phone some months later. He had called to tell me that he was looking to start a line of anthologies under the poetry imprint at Fitzhenry & Whiteside – something along the lines of the series of personal anthologies edited by Faber authors for that press: Alice Oswald's *The Thunder Mutters: 101 Poems for the Planet*, Sean O'Brien's and Don Paterson's *Train Songs: Poetry of the Railway*. I proposed myth poetry as a possible focus. Jones – a myth poet himself, for my money, as well as a critic and editor – agreed to co-edit. The process has been, in part, a conversation with Jones about what myth poetry is – about how it persists, and why.

In 2010, the Newfoundland poet Mark Callanan (b. 1979) published a chapbook entitled *Sea Legend*. On the cover is an enigmatic mermaid. A central figure in this chapbook-collection, she reappears in Callanan's 2011 book *Gift Horse*, with sisters:

> With combs carved from porpoise jaws,
> they rake their seaweed tangles out
> and coif their hair like centrefolds
> at a poolside party on the rocks.

In another poem she is pulled from the sea – dead, but briefly risen to confound the fishermen:

> They drew her up among the tons of codfish,
> a pair of glistening pearl studs at each ear....

And in still another, "Whitbourne's Mermaid," she appears on the tongue of one Captain Whitbourne, who might, in another time and place, be called the last mythopoet:

She was visible for a moment only,
long enough the captain knew
for certain that he'd seen her:

her breasts like delicate sand dollars,
a wake of hair trailing down her neck;
more girl in form than woman, really.

But that beauty, that rare creature
must have recognized something
wolfish in his gaze, for she turned

tail and buried herself beneath
the waves. Rumour has it
he followed and caught her,

emerged stark naked and dripping water,
praising sea legends
and the siren's element.

Though, once, while liquored up
on heavy grog and singing
every ballad we could think of,

he confessed the seam of her dive
was a quiet furrow, a locked oyster shell
and other veiled analogies.

I have wrestled with that "veiled analogies": grain of sand in a nacreous poem. Isn't *any* analogy a kind of veil – at once concealing and revealing what it purports to describe? Yet these are not "veiling analogies"; they are "veiled analogies." How so? The two analogies that Callanan gives us are hardly veiled: both vehicle and tenor are clearly stated – though we may guess that, in these cases, both vehicle and tenor veil a third thing, a hidden tenor,

11

sexual and/or sacred in nature. But apparently Whitbourne has offered other "veiled analogies," beyond these two: we are left to speculate as to what they might be. The effect of that "veiled," which begs so many questions, is to cast a veil over the whole of the poem, making me wonder if the poem is *itself* a veiled analogy, an elaborate vehicle for an unstated, perhaps unstatable, tenor.

Callanan's mermaids are descendants of Newfoundland sea-myths and Water-Street whores – but they are also descendants of the mermaids that haunted an earlier generation of myth poets. Here is Macpherson's "Mermaid":

> The fish-tailed lady offering her breast
> Has nothing else to give.
> She'll render only brine, if pressed,
> That none can drink and live.
>
> She has a magic glass, whose spell
> Makes bone look wondrous white.
> By day she sings, though, travellers like to tell,
> She weeps at night.

And here is Richard Outram's (1930-2005) "Mermaid" – the third section of his poem of that title, from the 1975 collection *Turns and Other Poems:*

> Though I was constantly caressed,
> Slow wave on wave,
> No infant suckled my salt breast:
>
> And I was wracked with every tide:
> And saw your sail
> And offered you an ardent bride:
>
> O Mariner, forgive those arts,
> That sensual song,
> That promised you true woman's parts:

> An ocean shuddered as we cleaved:
> Hot flesh: cold fish:
> A mortal drowned: a Child conceived!

It seems that every generation needs to catch the mermaid for itself. And every generation finds her not quite catchable: her dive a quiet furrow, as Callanan says (verses are furrows, etymologically speaking), a locked oyster shell. True union – hot flesh: cold fish – leaves the mortal dead, or the mermaid dead, or some of each, even as various children, and poems, are conceived.

Thinking about the mermaid makes me wonder if every myth poet is in some sense the last myth poet: poets, at least in our time and place, tend to preside over the moment when myth dies – or rather, when it passes out of the realm of the mythological and into the realm of the personal.

Here is David Greene, Professor of Celtic Studies, in a 1973 panel discussion on the theme of "Ancient Myth and Poetry":

> Even before Hugh McGuire had become chief of his name [the Irish poet] Eochaidh had written personal poems to him in which he demonstrated his special friendship for the man; that is to say, he spoke to him not in the correct traditional terms in which it is right to speak to a reigning prince, as a man wedded to his kingdom, but he spoke to him in personal terms, as a friend. This, of course, was a terrible break with the tradition. We can see now that as society decays, personal poetry advances.
>
> The myth is to some extent decaying and the personal poet appears.... [A]fter that you can find the situation in which a poet will pick up some pieces of the myth of the past, what was a coherent and unifying force, and use them for poetical purposes.

Is the myth poet like the holographer who, in Steven Heighton's (b. 1961) poem "Rewriting the Dead," flashes a hologram on the sky "at the moment the Pharoahs' star blinks out" – an eraser of myth, even as he or she purports to preserve it?

What Greene sees as the death of myth could be conceived of as its revivification, however. Here is Macpherson, speaking as part of that same 1973 panel discussion: "I think that a mythology that is no longer capable of change and absorbing new layers of possibility is a dead one that can only be studied from books." So when a poet like Patrick Anderson transposes the Persephone myth into wintry Montreal (Macpherson takes his poem "Winter in Montreal" as her case study), what Macpherson sees is not the death of the myth but rather "its stability, its durability, [and] also its metamorphic power, the protean flexibility and, if one can say it, venerean openness that has belonged to the life of such elements since they were fully released from religion into art."

So poets are, if not myth's stewards, its carriers – the way human beings can carry, all unbeknownst to them, a virus or a gene: the more we try to catch the mermaid, the more she catches us.

In his 1984 lecture "The Koine of Myth," Frye writes: "The word *myth* is used in such a bewildering variety of contexts that anyone talking about it has to say first of all what his chosen context is." For Frye, whose chosen context was literary criticism, "myth always [meant], first and primarily, *mythos,* story, plot, narrative." Insofar as myth is simply the narrative element in literature, the story of myth poetry is the story of poets' fascination with story itself, from Classical accounts of gods and monsters, to the genesis stories of science and religion, to literary narratives, to pop-culture anecdotes. (Macpherson calls myth, very broadly, "any element in literature that has the effect of enlarging a work's scope beyond the merely descriptive.")

Poetry and story are cognate, of course, or seem to be. The earliest poems we know *are* stories: the *Iliad,* the *Odyssey,* the epic of Gilgamesh. When written-down poems move from the epic mode into the lyric mode they become something different: they move, perhaps, away from story, and in the direction of art or music. (For all we know, this may be a move back, as opposed to a move forward: poetry may have begun in unrecorded worlds that are more visual or musical than they are narrative – but that's over the horizon, beyond what we can see.)

But lyric poems – contemporary, written-down lyric poems – retain their fascination with narrative. And it is perhaps precisely at the point that poets move away from the longer forms we associate with epic, and toward the shorter, lyric modes, that myths in the sense of canonical stories, stories recognized within a culture by certain basic and recurring elements, become most useful to poets: because this kind of story can be referenced in a phrase, a word. The part evokes the whole. Thus when Jason Guriel (b. 1978) ends his poem "Alchemy" with the words

> ... So many things
> you think are Prince Hals
> are really just kings.

we can hear behind them not only Shakespeare's history plays, in which Prince Hal figures, but the story of the frog prince (to be fair, Guriel sets this up with wand and wart references in his opening lines – but the frog is there for me, in his closing lines, regardless) and, behind that, the Classical stories of transformation, of mistaken identity: chief among them, perhaps, the story of another frog prince, the beggar-king Ulysses. For a lyric poet, a master of economy, this kind of thing is incomparable bang for your buck, and goes no small way toward explaining myth's formal fascination. (Of course, Homer knew this too: see the many glancing references to *other* stories, embedded within his stories of Troy and travel. Economy is not merely the province of the lyricist.)

But as Frye reminds us, the word "myth" has another sense, which goes beyond "story," or even "canonical story":

Two categories of stories crystallize in most societies. At the center is a body of "serious" stories: they may be asserted to have really happened, but what is important about them is not that, but that they are stories which it is particularly urgent for the community to know. They tell us about the recognized gods, the legendary history, the origins of law, class structure, kinship formations, and natural features. These stories do not as a rule differ in structure from other stories that are told simply for entertainment, but they have a different social function.

A Christian reader – or one grown up in a society where Christianity predominates, as religion – might think, reading Guriel's poem, of yet another frog-prince, the gardener-"Master" Jesus Christ, appearing to Mary Magdalene at the entrance to the tomb.

So the story of myth poetry is also the story of poets' fascination with the gods. And I mean gods here in the broadest sense. Joseph Campbell writes, "It would not be too much to say that myth is the secret opening through which the inexhaustible energies of the cosmos pour into human cultural manifestations." When I say gods I mean something like, "the inexhaustible energies of the cosmos": I am talking about the traffic of earth and heaven, here – to put it in the terms of our anthology's title.

This is an anthology of Canadian myth poetry, broadly defined, and its quadripartite structure is informed by what Macpherson and Frye present as "the mythological framework of Western culture": the Judeo-Christian and Classical myths. In both ways, it reflects the literary worlds in which its editors are (pardon the pun) best versed. But ultimately, to see myth poetry as a tradition that is broad and vital, as opposed to narrow and moribund, means recognizing first that it is a phenomenon not merely of Canadian poetry but of poetry at large (good recent scholarship on mid-century Canadian myth poetry – see Melissa Dalgleish's "Frye

Unschooled" – has linked it not simply to Frye's criticism, for instance, but to the broader context of modern mythography: Eliot, Joyce, Yeats ...) – and second that myth itself is a phenomenon not merely of the Greek and Judeo-Christian contexts that were central to Frye, but of culture at large. So, when we think about Canadian myth poets, we want to think not only of poets working in the biblical and Classical traditions, but of poets working with indigenous myth (Robert Bringhurst), with various Islamic traditions (P.K. Page, Eric Ormsby), with Nordic myth (George Johnston or, in a later generation, Jeramy Dodds), with Hinduism (Outram) or Zen (Sanger) ...

I see that I have reached first for the names of poets who are to some extent outside of the mythological traditions on which they draw ("late at the feast," as Sanger puts it in his afterword to Bringhurst's *Ursa Major)*. Macpherson talks about the "venerean openness that has belonged to the life of [myth] since [it was] fully released from religion into art." Not all myth has been released in this way: what myths are "open" will vary hugely not only from culture to culture but from person to person. Thus for me, the unchurched child of a-religious parents, the Bible stories are fair game in a way that for a devout Christian like, say, Margaret Avison (1918-2007), they might not be. Which is not to say that Avison didn't write some spectacular mythopoeic poems – but for me the most memorable of them, actually (I'm thinking of the Dylanesque "Birth Day," included here), date from before her conversion.

It is uncomfortable to think that myth poets are inevitably appropriators, by vocation. "Appropriation of voice" is an academic bugbear: how much worse, then, appropriation of story? Yet I can't quite escape the conclusion. Sanger and Bringhurst are "myth poets," in the way I've been using that term, in a way that the aboriginal mythtellers whose work they have written about (and in Bringhurst's case translated), don't seem to be. These aboriginal mythtellers speak from a place in which story and poetry are one – the sort of place that David Greene evokes when he talks about the world of the Irish poet Eochaidh, before its fall into secularity.

Or do they?

Bringhurst's Haida mythtellers, like Sanger's Mi'kmaq mythteller Susan Barss, lived, as did Eochaidh, at a moment when the myth *was* "to some extent decaying," as Greene puts it – when the fabric of the culture out of which the myth grew, and which was, in turn, shaped by it, had been gravely damaged by violence, disease. This is the very moment at which myth poetry tends to flower. (In fact, Bringhurst gives a brilliant account of the way in which Skaay of the Qquuna Qiighawaay may be using a story he tells to slyly school his non-Native interlocutor: he is passing along a tradition, yes, but he is also playing on it, using it to speak to an occasion that is both contemporary and personal.)

How far back would we have to go to find a poet who predated myth poetry: who spoke out of the world of myth, tout court? Or rather, out of a world in which poetry and myth have not been separated – in which myth has not at all been released, as Macpherson puts it, by religion into art?

Perhaps it is not a matter of time. The doubter in me (or is it the believer?) suspects that doubt has always existed, alongside faith, its correlate and necessary counterpart, even in so-called "primary" societies (that word is Greene's, borrowed from Frank O'Connor). If this is the case, then myth poets have probably always existed, too, dancing about the fringes of religion, presiding over the entry of the sacred into the secular – yet also, paradoxically, ensuring the continuance of the sacred by way of its secular immersions. And if myth poetry has always existed, perhaps the reverse is also true: perhaps even now in our secular age there are poets to whom it is given, every now and again, against all odds, to speak out of a world in which, as Sanger puts it in his essay "The Crooked Knife," "speech, myth, and music are synonymous."[1]

---

[1] I see now that the word "appropriation" is something of a red herring, and one that threatens to lead me into the rabbit warren (herring weir?) of identity politics. I want to talk about myth poetry not as the province of "outsiders" *or* "insiders," but rather as

The matter of immersion – the sacred in the secular, the secular in the sacred – brings us back to mermaids. In Callanan's account, Whitbourne is rumoured to have emerged from his salty rendezvous, "stark naked and dripping water, / praising sea legends / and the siren's element." Encounters with the siren's element don't always go so well, however. I think of Heighton's approximation (his word) of the Horatian ode to Pyrrha, *"Quis multa gracilis te puer in rosa ...."* (There is something mythopoeic about any "approximation" – the translated poem being, to some extent, the translator's myth, presenting competing obligations, of fidelity, of resistance.) Heighton titles his poem simply "Pyrrha" – a reminder not only of the Horatian femme fatale but of the mother of humanity, Deucalion's wife, one of the two human survivors of Jove's flood:

> What slender elegant youth, perfumed
> among roses, is urging himself on you,
>   Pyrrha, in the fragrant grotto? Have you
>   bound your yellow hair so gracefully
>
> for him? How many times he'll weep because
> faith is fickle, as the gods are, how often
>   will the black, sea-disquieting winds
>   astonish him, although for now
>
> credulous, grasping at fool's gold, he enjoys you,
> hopes you'll always be calm water, always
>   this easy to love. Unconscious of the wind's wiles
>   he's helpless, still tempted

---

a genre distinct from, though related to, devotional poetry. It is tempting to say that, if devotional poetry is the poetry of faith, then myth poetry is the poetry of doubt. But more what I mean is that myth poetry – whether written by one apparently outside or apparently inside a cultural group or faith tradition – is written from that place of openness that Macpherson describes. (In his essay "The Meaning of Mythology," Bringhurst writes: "Because mythologies and sciences alike aspire to be true, they are perpetually under revision. Both lapse into dogma when this revision stops.")

> by your gleaming seas. But high on the temple wall
> I've set this votive tablet, and in thanks
> to the god for rescue have hung
> my sea-drenched mantle there.

Ovid's Pyrrha, the flood-survivor, would seem to be the opposite of a mermaid: she is a symbol for the high and dry. But Heighton's Pyrrha, like Horace's, *is* the sea – its gleaming waters as tempting as any siren, and as dangerous. The poet who has survived his encounter with her must give thanks. He leaves as offering his sea-drenched mantle – and also "this votive tablet" (the demonstrative pronoun is by no means standard in translations of this ode): that is to say, this poem.

It seems to me that the great myth poems are precisely this: a record of immersion; a boast of survival; the fulfilment of a vow (votive, from the Latin *votum,* a vow or wish); an expression of thanks; a warning.

In a gloss on his own translation of the Pyrrha ode, David West writes:

> When Greeks or Italians retired, they might dedicate the tools of their trade in the temple of the appropriate god. The fisherman might hang up his nets, the gladiator a wooden spear, the courtesan her mirror. Saved from shipwreck, they might offer up the clothes they had been washed ashore in.

What might the poet dedicate? His or her poems, those sea-drenched words, hoping that they will prove to be worth their salt.

Works Cited

Bringhurst, Robert. "The Meaning of Mythology." *Everywhere Being Is Dancing: Twenty Pieces of Thinking.* Kentville, NS: Gaspereau Press, 2007. 63-72.

–. *A Story as Sharp as a Knife: The Classical Haida Mythtellers and Their World.* 2nd ed. Vancouver, BC: Douglas & McIntyre, 2011.

Callanan, Mark. *Gift Horse.* Montréal, QC: Signal Editions, 2011.

–. *Sea Legend.* Victoria, BC: Frog Hollow Press, 2010.

Dalgleish, Melissa. "Frye Unschooled: Mythopoeic Modernism in Canada." *English Studies in Canada* 37.2 (2011): 43-66.

Frye, Northrop. "The Koine of Myth: Myth as a Universally Intelligible Language." *Myth and Metaphor: Selected Essays 1974-1988.* Ed. Robert D. Denham. Charlottesville, VA: University Press of Virginia, 1990. 3-17.

– and Jay Macpherson. *Biblical and Classical Myths: The Mythological Framework of Western Culture.* Toronto, ON: University of Toronto Press, 2004.

Greene, David, Jay Macpherson, et al. "Ancient Myth and Poetry: A Panel Discussion." *Myth and Reality in Irish Literature.* Ed. Joseph Ronsley. Waterloo, ON: Wilfrid Laurier University Press, 1977. 1-16.

Guriel, Jason. "Alchemy." *Pure Product.* Montréal, QC: Signal Editions, 2009. 15.

Heighton, Steven. "Pyrrha." *The Address Book: poems.* Toronto, ON: House of Anansi Press, 2004. 72.

–. "Rewriting the Dead." *The Ecstasy of Skeptics: poems.* Concord, ON: House of Anansi Press, 1994. 37.

Jones, Evan. "We Need to Talk About Canada." *PN Review* 211 (2013): 55-8.

Macpherson, Jay. *Poems Twice Told:* The Boatman *and* Welcoming Disaster. Toronto, ON: Oxford University Press, 1981.

Outram, Richard. "Mermaid." *Turns and Other Poems.* London, UK / Toronto, ON: Chatto & Windus with the Hogarth Press / Anson-Cartwright Editions, 1975/6.

Sanger, Peter. "The Crooked Knife." *Spar: Words in Place*. Kentville, NS: Gaspereau Press, 2002. 27-36.

–. "Late at the Feast: An Afterword." *Ursa Major: A Polyphonic Masque for Speakers & Dancers,* by Robert Bringhurst. Kentville, NS: Gaspereau Press, 2003.

–. *White Salt Mountain: Words in Time*. Kentville, NS: Gaspereau Press, 2005.

West, David. *Horace Odes I: Carpe Diem*. Oxford, UK: Clarendon Press, 1995.

Earlier versions of this essay were delivered as a talk for the literary table of the Arts & Letters Club of Toronto, 1 April 2014, and published in *PN Review* 219 (September/October 2014).

Evan Jones
Earth and Heaven: An Introduction

It was in D.J. Enright's anthology *Poets of the 1950s* that Philip Larkin (1922-1985) first delivered his provocative "myth-kitty" pronouncement: "As a guiding principle I believe that every poem must be its own sole freshly created universe, and therefore have no belief in 'tradition' or a common myth-kitty." This was, at arm's length, typical reactionary troublemaking from Larkin. He was forever responding to modernism in such terms – in this case to its reliance and overreliance on myth as foundation and intertextual reference. Think of *Ulysses, The Waste Land,* the Surrealist magazine *Minotaure*. Everyone was in on the game. And Larkin was never a team player. One of the problems with his statement, though, is that Larkin uses the language of myth to dismiss it. To declare a poem "its own sole freshly created universe" is to mythologize: all mythologies begin with a creation story.

Larkin would hate the comparison, but his words recall those of the Greek Nobel Laureate in poetry Odysseas Elytis (1911-1996), who "kept the mechanism of myth-making but not the figures of mythology" in his own work. Larkin, whether he liked it or not, was interested in myth-making – even if not the famous myths. "The Whitsun Weddings" is mythopoeic; "Church Going" is mythopoeic. Yet both poems avoid the figures and the archetypes of what we traditionally define as mythology. Sort of.

I suppose at the heart of this, it's easiest to suggest that there's myth and then there's *myth*. Larkin's argument, as he clarified in his 1982 *Paris Review* interview, was "in support of provincialism." Elytis was much more interested in connecting with the continuum of the Western tradition. The difference between them isn't as severe as it might seem. Both men reached out from their local surroundings to the larger world by considering the particular in their poetry. So, it's best perhaps to view them as opposite ends of the same spectrum: Larkin's provincial myth at one end, Elytis's continual myth at the other.

Archetypal myth is far from the dominant theme, in our era, that it was for the modernists. The modernists in all their guises drew on myth so heavily we might think they drove it underground. Michael Bell has argued that they sought in myth "a mode of self-grounding," many turning their backs on centuries of literature focused on metaphysical problems in favour of myth. Yes and no. It's difficult to generalize about the modernists, much as we might like to. And so much of myth is linked to the metaphysical that the argument seems to oversimplify. But Bell does make a valid point about self-grounding. Any poet of significance begins with a foundation, both physical and mythical/metaphysical.

In this book, you will find Eve admiring a garden snake, Lot's wife prowling George Street, toy merchants hawking Trojan horses, a poet setting sail for Babylon. There are poems about gods and tricksters, ravens and pigs' ears. All of them contain pieces from larger, older narratives, which are brought together by a Canadian poet in a new pattern or form. And now they are assembled here, editorially, in yet another pattern: a movement from creation through to apocalypse and/or afterlife; a narrative; a story that my co-editor and I are trying to tell you.

In arranging the poems we have followed Jay Macpherson's "four phases" from her book *Four Ages of Man: The Classical Myths,* published in 1962: "creation and the coming of the gods; pastoral life and the ordering of the seasons; the adventures and the labours of the heroes; war, tragic tales, and decline into history." Our section headings are selected from amongst hers, each corresponding with one of the four phases she describes: our section "In the Beginning" is foundational, poets setting up universes and starting points; "Loves of the Gods and Metamorphoses" looks at the connections and disjunctions between humans and gods, the dead and the living; "The Heroes" is about those who are, or would seek to be, god-like on Earth; "The Passing and Afterlife of the Gods" is the apocalypse, life after the end – or perhaps it simply gestures towards where we might sail next. Macpherson's work has served since our early discussions as a genesis in itself for our thinking, and it seemed fitting to both follow her example and pay tribute in this way.

This anthology features poems that tie into various longer and larger narrative continua. Yes, you might need a dictionary of mythology, access to the internet, a little bit of patience. The poems don't expect you to know everything, but they do hope – as we do – that you will look things up (though even looking things up will not always tell you *why* a poet is citing a myth). Guilty as charged, Mr. Larkin. But then, no poem can contain itself. Just using the language connects to a larger world. How can one be narcissistic without Narcissus? Cyclopean without the Cyclops? Cunning without Odysseus?

We chose the poems because our aim is to tell a story, using the best methods available to us. We argued, discussed, manipulated, presented, and came up with a list that pleases us both. There are others whose work we might have included and even thought of including: both poets for whom myth poetry is a major mode (Margaret Atwood, Anne Carson, D.G. Jones, Eli Mandel ...) and those who drew our attention with one great mythopoeic poem or sequence. Poems by John Barton, Don Coles, Crispin Elsted, Jason Guriel, Anita Lahey, Ross Leckie, Michael Lista, Nyla Matuk, George Murray, Jena Schmitt, Todd Swift and many others wound up on our cutting-room floor – not ultimately because we didn't like them, but because we were trying to fashion a narrative arc. We wanted to make an anthology that an interested reader might read in a single sitting. We were not trying to construct a compendium, still less a historical portrait of myth poetry in this country.

This is, importantly, 'an' anthology, not 'the'. It's our personal guide to the kind of mythic world in which Amanda and I have become poets. It's a survey and a study, a guide and reference. We want to draw attention to a part of the tradition that has fallen by the wayside, slipped out of fashion and into critical neglect.

Twentieth-century Canadian myth poetry is usually considered in the light of Northrop Frye's work and his influence on a generation which has now passed. It was that generation I was thinking of when I wrote that Amanda was "the last mythopoet." Daryl Hine had just died, Macpherson a few months before, and the illustrator and writer Virgil Burnett (as much a myth poet as any). This seemed to me the end of something. Amanda is right to correct me, though. Even as a historical school has ended, we look in this anthology beyond that school, to a larger sense of identity and connection.

Still, there is much work to be done on this subject, and a more definitive anthology is overdue. And not just of Frye-inspired work; rather, something historical that takes into consideration the many parallel traditions of myth poetry that are part of the Canadian imagination. *Earth and Heaven* is not that book. It is instead best read as the personal project Amanda describes in her preface. It is modern and contemporary, because that is where our interests lie. We have limited ourselves from the outset because of the form we drew from Macpherson, and so had to choose one Orpheus over another. We centred on English-language poetry. There is so much ground to cover that not focusing in this way would have kept us reading for years. Well, it *will* keep us reading for years. For now, these are the roots we have found, knowing there are more to find.

Works Cited

Bell, Michael. *Literature, Modernism and Myth: Belief and Responsibility in the Twentieth Century*. Cambridge, UK: Cambridge University Press, 2006.

Elytis, Odysseas. *Open Papers*. Translated by Olga Broumas and T. Begley. Port Townsend, WA: Copper Canyon Press, 1995.

Enright, D.J., ed. *Poets of the 1950s: An Anthology of New English Verse*. Tokyo, Jpn.: Kenkysha, 1955.

Larkin, Philip. Interview with Robert Philips, "The Art of Poetry No. 30." *The Paris Review* 84 (1982): http://www.theparisreview.org/interviews/3153/the-art-of poetry-no-30-philip-larkin.

Macpherson, Jay. *Four Ages of Man: The Classical Myths*. Toronto, ON: Macmillan, 1965.

Jay Macpherson
The Marriage of Earth and Heaven

Earth draws her breath so gently, heaven bends
On her so bright a look, I could believe
That the renewal of the world was come,
The marriage of kind Earth and splendid Heaven.

"O happy pair" – the blind man lifts his harp
Down from the peg – but wait, but check the song.
The two you praise still matchless lie apart,
Thin air drawn sharp between queen Earth and Heaven.

Though I stand and stretch my hands forever
Till my hair grows down my back and my skirt to my ankles,
I shall not hear the triumphs of their trumpets
Calling the hopeful in from all the quarters
To the marriage of kind Earth and splendid Heaven.

Yet out of reason's reach a place is kept
For great occasions, with a fat four-poster bed
And a revelling-ground and a fountain showering beer
And a fiddler fiddling fine for folly's children
To riot rings around at the famous wedding
Of quean Earth and her fancy-fellow Heaven.

I. In the Beginning

Harry Thurston
[Unknown]

We all must come from somewhere. Out of the blackness of time,
moon-faced, our complexions pocked by the catastrophe of
  beginnings.

Why not believe as did the ancient marsh dwellers?
The sacred ibis spoke the gods into being,

laying an egg from which the sun burst forth.
The rest is history. Or so said Herodotus.

It was the jet-black ibises, with their hooked beaks
down-turned like the nibs of pens, who gave us writing.

One story is as good as another.
We all must come from somewhere,

shining out of the blackness of time.
Believe what you must.

Daniel David Moses
Crow Out Early

The only one who speaks to this long rain
is that crow sitting on a pole like old
Raven, spitting out caws in pairs. He got
out of dreams on this wrong side of the bay.

Over there a foghorn makes a four-note
effort Crow can't comprehend. It's not like
even the loudest moans of his friends who
keep asleep, their effort to ignore how

this pressing fall of clouds has made a pine
the only place to settle. This makes Crow
with folded wings a black and glistening
pair of hands and his cries, a quick prayer, reach

out through the fog. His eyes get a shimmer
and his ears a song, both like the run off
gurgling at road edge. He sees the stones there
washing strong bodies egg bright, beetle slick.

Douglas LePan
River-God

There is water at my feet
Moving through the shadowed bridge.
It coils and melts in silence, glides
A monarch from the realm of darkness.

Where have I seen that same dark beauty,
The smooth glister along its back
So self-possessed and final? Where
Have I seen it trail its invitation?

It spreads slowly and broadens past
The arches, ample for any burden
To take and mingle with itself,
Yet goes straight on, makes no entreaty.

For what has it to do with me
Or with this city? It comes from caves
That we know nothing of, twisting
In reluctance from the earth,

And flows unmoved by midnight bells,
Listening to no sound except
Its own, seeing no other face,
While absent from its own dominion.

Gwendolyn MacEwen
Our Child Which Art in Heaven

The child leads the parents on to bear him; he demands
        to be born. And I sense somehow that God
Is not yet born; I want to create Him.

If everything were finished, and we could say
        we'd given birth to stars, if we could say
Give over, it's done – all would be wild, and fair.

But it is not yet over; it has not yet begun.

God is not yet born, and we await the long scream
        of His coming. We want the water to break
So we can say: *In the Beginning was the Word.*

Meanwhile, if one must die for something,
        there's nothing like the cross
from which to contemplate the world.

Margaret Avison
Birth Day

Saturday I ran to Mytilene.

Bushes and grass along the glass-still way
Were all dabbled with rain
And the road reeled with shattered skies.

Towards noon an inky, petulant wind
Ravelled the pools, and rinsed the black grass round them.

Gulls were up in the late afternoon
And the air gleamed and billowed
And broadcast flung astringent spray
                        All swordy-silver.
I saw the hills lie brown and vast and passive.

The men of Mytilene waited restive
Until the yellow melt of sun.
I shouted out my news as I sped towards them
That all, rejoicing, could go down to dark.

All nests, with all moist downy young
Blinking and gulping daylight; and all lambs
Four-braced in straw, shivering and mild;
And the first blood-root up from the ravaged beaches
Of the old equinox; and frangible robins' blue
Teethed right around to sun:
These first we loudly hymned;
And then
The hour of genesis
When first the moody firmament

Swam out of Arctic chaos,
Orbed solidly as the huge frame for this
Cramped little swaddled creature's coming forth
To slowly, foolishly, marvellously
Discover a unique estate, held wrapt
Away from all men else, which to embrace
Our world would have to stretch and swell with strangeness.

This made us smile, and laugh at last. There was
Rejoicing all night long in Mytilene.

SOUVANKHAM THAMMAVONGSA
The Bible, Notes On

I can only
read

one word
here

You put it
inside

a bracket
and

placed
it

above

George Johnston
Creation

for Gerald Trottier,
especially for his "Easter Series" paintings

You stand in your island studio,
a bare canvas big in front of you,
your thought big with what you mean to paint:
I blench to think what; my heart grows faint.

The thing itself, God's poor bare forked us,
creatures of God's hand, wilful, anxious,
at home and not at home anywhere
on bludgeoned earth, in envenomed air.

A while since, you painted a far green
country. Did you long for that serene?
Did you see the land of lost content,
or glimpse, perhaps, what Creation meant?

Fiat, fiat! the saint's driven cry:
you look at us as with the saint's eye,
fellow mortals in Creation's chance
the Word chose, and launched intelligence.

What courage we know we know by fear,
life by death, hope we know by despair.
Must it be so? Is our Paradise
without courage and hope, without price?

Sweet love and hate, pride and bitter fall:
what cost our Paradise, after all?
Are the losses that we suffer here
what make dear all that we hold most dear?

Grief we cannot seem to live without:
we make trouble when we have it not.
Direst horrors are those ourselves make:
are these also for Creation's sake?

John heard, Behold, I make all things new.
God with us did live our darkest through;
taught the word of love and no word wrote;
lived a book that warring sides may quote.

Children of that Life, how ought we pray?
What you paint, Gerald, is what you say,
and what you live, that too is your word:
all one word, with the Creator Word.

JOHN TERPSTRA
Genesis

Because the pain is exquisite and excruciating
when I merely graze my knee against the bird bath,
I bend to sit on a low branch of the apple tree
that graces this garden,
and hear a *thump,*
and turn to see her fallen on the ground.

Because we are so eager and afraid
for all the living things we have no names for,
that will bud and grow and require tending
in this spring of our new dominion,
we have woken early on this first warm weekend morning
to clip and till.

And it's good, working side by side.
We are happy how quickly the beds come clean.
We are doubly happy the raspberry patch,
whose pruning protocol the gardening book
confused for us all winter, revealed its needs
in our presence, its trim canes now poised to bear.

We bend and stand and bend again, and stay too long
in the sun. I graze my knee. She faints.
It's as though a variation on some ancient theme
is being played out. I brush particles of soil
from her face. She rises and goes indoors,
a slight bruise on her cheek.

Beverley Bie Brahic
PS: Book of Eve

    about that snake: it was beautiful,
    truly
        it was beautiful
    coiled on the cheek
    of rock in early sun.
    A garden snake, harmless therefore.
    Bronze, I recall, frieze
    of diamonds or black
    down its sides or back
    like great uncle Sandy's
    tartan socks.
    One of life's lords
    Granddad wrestled
    topsoil on his acre
    of paradise. Beyond cedars
    ocean sparkled. Stairs
    descended to the first bright
    beach of the world. Tide rising
    or falling. It glittered
    its tongue at me
    and I will never forget
    how it took me in, then
    sashayed off
    into the rough
    where the berries hung.

ANNE COMPTON
Birdlore

The Protestant revolution had its source in shipping.
    Christopher Skiff

The miserable raven returned over the water. Nowhere to light.
Valleys and fiords, forty days gone, recede in memory. His alto
of praise reduced to a croak – a voice grown hoarse in a further
removal from God. Earth in exile, as happened twenty-seven
    man-names before.

Back when it started, the leaves waxed with water, and his own
    sheen shinier,
delighted him. The showery odour of rose, looped with honey-
    suckle, seemed
a kind of vocality – scent and accent the same – and he its
    ventriloquist.

Unless angels singing their admiration reach us, beauty's forfeit.

He keeps this thought to himself. Day neither damp nor sun, the
    grey of it future imperfect.

Now that the rain's stopped, the man's chinsing the seams of the
    boat with bitumen. Rope
over the side. While he works, he calculates the likely rate of
    increase in the breeding stock,
sees how the cypress wood could be salvaged for a house on the
    hill. God's collaborator is

what he calls himself, raising a new world refreshed of sin. He's
   just reformed the word
calling, plans a trade for the boys, jobs for the wife. Grounded, he
   thinks, in work.

There's been no welcome. The man believes him a bird of ill habit.
He's already had a word with the dove. They're making history.

You think I don't know how a metaphor works through substance.

II. Loves of the Gods and Metamorphoses

ROBERT BRINGHURST
[from *Ursa Major*]

[Arcturus:]

Perfectly simple. One of the ones in the sky
wanted one of the ones on the ground.
And got what he wanted, as usual. Then
couldn't keep it. If they can't, who can?

What a way to find yourself a mother.
But what other way is better?
You can have what you want but can't have it for long.
That's the rule.
                Now the one on the ground –
that is, the one who found herself a mother –
was already in the service of another from the sky –
a woman from the sky who lived most of the year
on the ground. And that one chased her out
and damn near killed her, because she was impure.
Being a mother, you see, is impure. In some people's
thinking. Love is pure but loving isn't. Even thinking
about loving isn't pure, in some people's thinking.

Another woman from the sky – the first one's wife, of course –
came down and chased her too, until she – this is true –
she hid inside the ground.
                      One of the ones
in the sky wanted one of the ones
on the ground, and the wife of the one in the sky
chased the one on the ground until she went
into the ground like a bear, and that was where

she really did become a mother. That was where
she bore her child.
                      One of them loved her enough –
if love is what you call it – that he wanted her
up in the sky, and the other one hated her so much
that she wanted to bury her in the ground.
So there in the ground she gave birth
to the sky-father's child.
                      The one who fell
in love with her – if love is what you call it –
who had come around too early, came around again
too late and picked her up again
and lifted her into the sky. If you live on the ground
you can see her. Not from your cities, of course,
but from out on the prairie.
The ground is getting awfully bright these days.
In fact, it looks as though the people on the ground
want their places on the ground to be as bright
as anything in heaven.

DARREN BIFFORD
Wedding in Fire Country

We pretend the water bombers are buffalo
bellying the lake, which they slurp sloppily.

Sloppily we suck at our beers and cut into
my father's steaks. The fires in the mountains

are at first far enough away we don't notice them.
The smoke they issue is barely distinguishable

from the white clouds, except by the way it gathers
instead of dissipates, as clouds will do after storms.

I am here and you are comfortably beside me.
We've flown to our wedding and everyone is coming.

But the fire leapt the highway last night when we slept,
so this morning we drive to our ceremony by a longer route.

What a drive! No fires! Some cattle and a laundry place
that sells ice cream of which we heatedly partake.

The switchback back into the valley is cut
down a steep slope above which the trees turn

deciduous and weather patterns differ, being mainly more
turbulent and subject to rainstorms and thunder.

Here, below, we find the air dry as the patterns
in summer incline to sun and fire. It is summer.

We are here. Our families have gathered, plus friends.
I wake early and open the curtains to rosy mountains.

Smoke chugs into more of itself darkly enough to scare
my little cousin who wonders about our safety.

Her fear and joy are not at all wily. It's okay, I say.
It's no problem. But I sense she demands of herself that she accept

what I tell her and reject what she feels. Look, it's raining!
This is a fine thing, considering the fires. Under this umbrella

you are huddled in your white fine dress and our friends
are throwing wet confetti, and see! – there is my father

and your father joyous with one another. The father
of the hills is the sky, they say. The father

of the water is the river. The father of the buffalo
is the earth, which is the son of the hills, plus beard lichen.

The grandfather of the buffalo is therefore the sky.
Therefore the buffalo have a desire for the sky,

as like to almost-like, hankering for communion,
desire solely to know its own difference from itself.

I am the son of my father and you are the daughter of another.
There is a difference between us that is distinct from the troubles

of mountains and deer. Now here I am talking about deer.
We are distinct from the deer, who are the siblings

of the slender trees that are courted by the wind,
and when so courted, do not totally resist its ravishments.

The wind is close in kind to the breath of the sky,
which is all the extension but not the progeny of anything

other than itself. For the wind is the fury and the author
of the way your hair flirts by not staying in one place

but flits above your eyebrows and ears. I wish at this time
to be the courter of your hair and the comforter

of your whorled ears. For tonight we've sojourned
close in that place where the fire's herd freely roams.

Leonard Cohen
Song

My lover Peterson
He named me Goldenmouth
I changed him to a bird
And he migrated south

My lover Frederick
Wrote sonnets to my breast
I changed him to a horse
And he galloped west

My lover Levite
He named me Bitterfeast
I changed him to a serpent
And he wriggled east

My lover I forget
He named me Death
I changed him to a catfish
And he swam north

My lover I imagine
He cannot form a name
I'll nestle in his fur
And never be to blame.

Alfred Bailey
Gluskap's Daughter

While the
girl grew cold at
her door-flap the
feathery air went
small and fell
over the ground
under the spell.
Objects around,
chipmunk and fox –
not water beetles
nor the otter
nor the beaver-queen's
aqueous daughter.
They all swarm,
all water kind,
in stream, pond,
and beyond,
in the space outside the
      place where the girl's
eye stopped.

If she were able to
dislodge her
finger from the stuff that
slowed to a stop all around
and point at the porcupine's
quill device that
hung from the flap
it would shred in-
to fish scales.

Her eye would come unstuck,
the chipmunks' tails
would quiver, and the fox's jowl.
All earth and air creatures,
hare, badger, bat, owl,
would come unstuck
and forthwith resume
a waterkin stance,
and in the girl's brown pupil,
and at her finger,
they would begin to dance.

Diana Brebner
Frozen

Broken Aphrodite, in a field of snow
wonders how she came here
and where her body goes. Does it

piece together, shatter, flow? Does
it move across the field: glacier,
traveller, road? Her colours are

clean and Greek, white and blue,
but the blank light angles in
from the north, with a vengeance.

Is this a body, so frozen
the cold has snapped arm from
torso and buried her at

the knees, in snow? Or was she made,
from the beginning, of water?
A voice chants, like a dark chorus:

The solid state is transitory.
Embodiment never lasts past
the heat of passion. I turn

to you, neither goddess nor ice,
and remember that warnings abound
about the effects of warming, how

the progress of love is irreversible.
Love moves, with or without us. Love,
what a terrible choice, when

the last part of you that remains
is your face, wet, shining, and anywhere
I can touch you, we are melting.

Mary Dalton
Salt Mounds, St. John's Harbour

If Lot's wife were to lie flat on her back,
a giant salt woman sprawling at ease on the waterfront,
these would be her breasts –
these massive salt mounds
laced tight in their black vinyl tarps,
many-teated, studded with rings of battered old tires.
A two-domed harbinger of winter,
any day now she'll rouse herself, hoist up her bulk.
White-socketed, eyeless, she'll traipse up from the harbour.
She'll tramp the wry streets, on the prowl for
the blinking bright follies, the glitter of George Street.
Ceres' barren sister, she'll burn all she touches.
Where she walks: the skid and the squeal,
crumpled metal, broken hips, lost gloves,
black ice and blizzards,
the lanes crying their toxic brown slush,
the blundering snowploughs,
our tilting away from the sun.

Steven Heighton
Were You to Die

Were you to die I'd be free to go off
and see the world, and sleep in every elsewhere
I might never arrive
– yet I might choose to travel alone
from window to window looking out
on the streets of your city,
where your friends still expect to see you sometimes,
or mistake you for someone, out of custom – love –

Without your thrashing, manic dreams, my body
would sleep better
but wake more tired, I'd let the garden go to seed
the way I always meant to
and when I looked out the window into the yard
I'd never miss the snowpeas, beets and roses
but your sunhat I might miss – you hunkered down
in a summer dress, your fingers
grouped like roots in the raised beds,
your stooped, stubborn nape, your cinnamon-
freckled shoulders –

Were you to die, my heart
would be free to pack a bag
and book passage for the riot of islands
I might have been, and shared
with the one and numberless "beloved" we fumble
our whole lives glimpsing
a moment too late,
when Eden was always the one who stayed
rooted in her changes, and gave you

the island in her arms, and when you slept
somehow she travelled, and when you woke
she was changed –

Were you to die, my mind
would be free to twist inward
the way fingers fist, and fasten pat
on its own taut notions, theorems, palm shut fast
to the snow that pooled there and seemed to flow through
when the skin still flowered in fullest winter
and I loved you, and thoughts, like books,
were doors that opened outward
not coffins, closed,
not cells –

Were you to die and free me
my body would follow you down into the cold
prison of your passing, and warm you when all the others
had turned away, and try bribing
the keeper with a poem, or fool him
with keychains of chiming words – an elegy
so pure he'd be pressed to cry, eyes
thawing and the earth warmed, April
when rain falls like a ransom, through opened arms
that bore the sun down with you, warm.

Sue Sinclair
Orpheus Meets Eurydice in the Underworld

Still limping, she has come. She waits at the foot of the hill, doesn't dare go further, remembers how it once vanished under her feet.

She has spent the time thinking about her wedding day, tracing the mark on her ankle where the serpent bit. It hasn't healed yet; perhaps it won't until he comes back. She has never desired his death, but wished for it as one wishes for rain.

The steep hill, where it led and couldn't lead. So many times.

When he arrives he looks more tired than she can understand. The lyre has vanished; they stand together silently.

Even as she remembers his face, she loses something else. She has been alone so long now; how often she has stood here, how much she has wanted to climb.

She takes him home, puts him to bed, then slips in beside him. His childhood bed, too short for him now; they will have to find another.

They waken slowly. As ghosts they pass through each other's bodies, she puts her hand into his heart. He has been worried she would forget.

They play in the fields, run races, drift through tall grasses carelessly, as only those who have had to wait forever can. They have a private sign language; no one speaks in this place, even the streams are still.

Sometimes when they are walking she teases him, falls behind. He looks over his shoulder again and again: there she is. They never tire of this game.

Robert Gibbs
Depth of Field

Through my camera's dead set
you come clear yet some ways vaguer
than those trees behind you
yellowing silver poplars out of focus

Pinned to my long eye
matched line to line across a hairsbreadth
you're losing sight for me and touch
lengthening armslengths

And at my dark eye's end
I've lit this ikon limned wholly
in blue and gold outside my own kind
or yours of seeing and being

What cheer is there in making it –
you – a Eurydice girl who went
underground too soon
and passed beyond blackness

way out in front?
Beautiful? Yes, more than ever
by any hard standard
fixed that way

composing a ghost, no two
laying them I'll say
by settling our love
bodydeep in outside ground

Bruce Taylor
Orphée

The time I bought a full-length mirror,
it barely fit in the car.
I had to pull the booster chair,
uproot the headrests
and recline the seat to lay it flat
like a long unbending body
rectangled in black,
with its feet toward the back.

It was a good passenger,
no trouble at all.
At every stop light I would look
over my shoulder at it,
and each time it was just lying there,
stiff as a pharaoh,
looking up through the sunroof at nothing,
at whatever was above us in the sky
as we went by.

Prone, with the long clouds
dashing across it, a mirror
is a little like a girl
lying in the sun,
and also a little like
the swimming pool she is beside,
with that deepening calm just under
the restless surface,
where the searching and elastic light
relaxes into settled blue.
I think the girl is you.

Now it stands in the bedroom,
remembering those clouds,
and reflecting on the day
of its abduction, when it lay
for nearly an hour in the glare
under the great, harsh sun
and gathered every bit of it in
and gave every bit of it back.
Before the new life began,
in the dim room
with the curtains drawn,
and the man who comes to stare
at something he wants in there.

Peter Sanger
After Monteverdi

All the true sounds descended to fetch her back,
    water the first with a dapping
of waves upon pebbles and wind she remembered
    filling through riverside spruce
those seafalls which fell between silence.
    She listened, listened,
heard the gather again into fullness
    and fall while a loon's dark
tremulant echoed itself over water,
    whickering close and away
before she could ask that it stop where it was,
    calling inside her. There
from the spruce, a ratchety burr, a clucking
    of truculent squirrels, elsewhere,
jay clack, heron screik, creak of crow wings
    oaring air, a whistle
of black duck circling the old green skiff
    which puddered slicked Acheron.
And next she could see him, ahead at the prow,
    his voice singing mutely, his hands
plucking notes from strings which vibrated in stillness.
    Wordless for now, she begged that he
listen to all the true sounds descending
    to fetch her back, but he sailed
his ceiling of water, his face looking up at his face
    drawing breath with the mouth
of things, and he couldn't just then turn to hear her.

MARK CALLANAN
The Myth of Orpheus

And I came to in a room with a draft
that issued from beneath a swinging door,
my head plugged up like a sink stuffed
with months of shed hair,
shaving stubble, other things
that thought to disappear.

And the covers were bunched
at my waist like a marble effigy
of Christ newly sprung from the cross,
unveiling an inch of midriff,
my navel, which in the hospital light
looked like a wound from a hollow-point.

And the old man in a nearby bed
kept dying. The monitor would shriek
its air raid warning and he would die
and come back. That was his trick.
He did it and did it. The slap-slap
of the nurses' soles was deliberate

applause. Then he left for good.
My wife said that when I was dead,
or during my death, she paced the garden
with my jacket on, cupping votive flames
to cigarettes. She killed each
match with a flick of her wrist,

then laid the burnt corpses to rest
in a packet scored with scratches
from matchstick heads that sought
to light the way, and did, and died.
Tendrils of smoke grew into the sky
as vines climbing from tomblike shade.

She stood, then, and helped me to my feet,
led me down the corridor
to find a cup of tea – past an orderly
who wheeled an assemblage
of bed, old woman, and IV –
not looking back to see if I was there.

III. The Heroes

Elise Partridge
Sisyphus: The Sequel

You pushed it up the hill every day.
Shoved your shoulder against it, sprained
your back.
Finding indentations on its surface,
you dug your fingernails in till they bled.
You invented a device to nudge it
                                      up.
Tried to hire a mercenary to
heave it.

And every day the stone trailed you down.
Some days, bouncing,
it taunted you. Often it pursued
you like a Fury,
a one-rock avalanche.

You begged it for mercy,
sat on it, ate on it, spat on it.
More than once you thought,
"let it crush me."

But gradually, grudging,
you began to ease it tenderly.
Its freckles you knew like a face's.
Your calling was to take it in your arms.

One dusk you crouched,
bracing yourself
for the bound back down.
A minute passed

as you massaged your calves, hardly noticing.
Five minutes, six –
you hauled yourself over the crest beside it,
laid your palms against it like a physician.
Suspiciously you waited.
                    It didn't move.

Afraid of letting one flare of hope char you,
        you huddled below.

It sat immobile
for hours, a
new-laid egg.

At dawn, you started to laugh.
        Flopped sideways, weak with laughter.

Days later, tapping crisply with a chisel,
you slice a hunk, striped with agony's chevrons.

DARYL HINE
Patroclus Putting on the Armour of Achilles

How clumsy he is putting on the armour of another,
His friend's, perhaps remembering how they used to arm each
    other,
Fitting the metal tunics to one another's breast
And setting on each other's head the helmet's bristling crest.
Now for himself illicitly he foolishly performs
Secret ceremonial with that other's arms,
Borrowed, I say stolen, for they are not his own,
On the afternoon of battle, late, trembling, and alone.

Night terminal to fighting falls on the playing field
As to his arm he fastens the giant daedal shield.
A while the game continues, a little while the host
Lost on the obscure littoral, scattered and almost
Invisible, pursue the endless war with words
Jarring in the darkening air impassable to swords.

But when he steps forth from the tent where Achilles broods
Patroclus finds no foe at hand, surrounded by no gods.
Only the chill of evening strikes him to the bone
Like an arrow piercing where the armour fails to join,
And weakens his knees under the highly polished greaves.
Evening gentle elsewhere is loud on the shore, it grieves
It would seem for the deaths of heroes, their disobedient graves.

Don McKay
Fates Worse Than Death

Atrocity
implies an audience of gods.
The gods watched as swiftfooted
godlike Achilles cut behind the tendons of both feet
and pulled a strap of oxhide through
so he could drag the body of Hektor,
tamer of horses, head down in the dust
behind his chariot.
Some were appalled, some not,
having nursed their grudges well, until
those grudges were fine milkfed
adolescents, armed
with automatic weapons. The gods,
and farther off,
the gods before the gods, those who ate
their children and contrived
exquisite tortures in eternity, watched
and knew themselves undead. Such is the loss, such
the wrath of swiftfooted godlike
Achilles, the dumb fucker, that he drags,
up and down, and round and round the tomb
of his beloved, the body of Hektor,
tamer of horses. Atrocity
is never senseless. No. Atrocity is dead ones
locked in sense, forbidden
to return to dust, but scribbled in it,
so that everyone – the gods,
the gods before the gods, the enemy, the absent mothers, all
must read what it is like to live out exile on the earth
without it, to be without recesses, place,

a campsite where the river opens
into the lake, must read
what it means to live against the sun and not to die.
Watch,
he says, alone in the public
newscast of his torment, as he
cuts behind the tendons of both feet,
and pulls a strap of oxhide through,
so he can drag the body that cannot stop being Hektor,
tamer of horses, head down in the dust
behind his chariot, watch
this.

Jeffery Donaldson
Troy

Eight centuries before
the common era, outside
the walls of a later Troy,

toy merchants hawked models
of the Trojan Horse,
and the children cried for them.

Centuries earlier, the gates
of Ilium were breached
when the colossal toy,

rumbling, was trotted in,
a winner's trophy, almost a gift,
until from the underside

spilled the tin soldiers
who cut open the children
crying inside the walls.

Marius Kociejowski
Coast

1

We moved among delicate instruments,
Taking for a theme the sovereign light,
The scrimshaw, the parliament of water.
We then sought a division between things.

Once divided, truth divides forever.

We abandoned the angelic forms, smashed
Against the wood our heavenly quadrant,
Struck aimlessly from island to island.

2

We embraced without shame what was simple.
We wept to see the wild geese heading home,
The small blue flowers we could never name,
The women so ripe in their summer clothes.

The compass we held true is stopped inside.

We worship as pure the broken circle.
A blind foghorn sounds our way toward shore,
The old bleached houses dispossessed of love.

3

A band marching in circles slays a tune.
A megaphone blares garlands of welcome.
What should we return to, and what survives
Of love? And who are the boys skipping stones?

The shallow waters keep our image moored.

We were proud scavengers once, and we come
As ghosts here, savages brandishing grace,
With nothing to give but this our silence.

4

Speak kindly of those we have abandoned,
The innocent who in their madness strayed,
Who mistook for seraphim a bright lamp
Beneath the waters camouflaging death.

Such tenderness the depths would not abide.

There was nothing could be done to save them.
We trembled as the gulls swallowed their cries,
And as the distance took what else remained.

5

Who shall carry them across the harbour,
These stranger particles that seek congress?
We say words alone keep our nature whole
Against the hard weathering of fractions.

So what now siphons our breath from inside?

There is no way home, and the petty schemes
Are brushed aside, and the horoscopes too,
The mock images, the lights on the shore.

6

As with fish entering the broken hulls
Or the blind eel tunnelling through the weed,
So shall we make darkness our corridor.
We will by dead reckoning tempt fortune.

Go, catch the slightest air should any come.

It is better so than light which is false,
Better the rougher shape, the ruined voice.
Ask nothing more, as more would madden us.

RICARDO STERNBERG
[from *Map of Dreams*]

No sooner had we left
the coastal waters,

the familiar latitudes,
than we were lost.

Rum-drunk, the captain
had himself blessed

and strapped to the mast
from where he begged to hear

something from the sirens.
Sail by power of dreams,

they crooned, *by ignoring maps,
by letting the helm* go.

When our supplies dwindled
we became desperate

and hammered our crosses
into crescent moons.

But neither cross nor moon
could replace the charts

the captain had destroyed.
We sailed as we could:

now for the sake of sailing
the silk sheen of this sea,

its blue susurrus.

Michael Crummey
Odysseus as a Boy

He's just tied his sitter to a chair
when the telephone rings in the kitchen –

a call for her, of course, and he flays
at the clumsy knots, red-handed, red-faced,

the teen shouting toward the receiver
to say she's coming and urging him on

in a whisper. He's not quite seven,
precociously horny, and embarrassed

to find himself roped to that mast
on such an oddly public stage,

so confounded he can't find the strand
that would lead him through the maze

contrived at each slender wrist.
The girl's fetching voice in his ear

insistent, pealing like a siren.

Richard Greene
St. Ignace

I

Though maps rendered the unknown as nothing,
this place, already made human by blood,
was made more so by an uncertain good:
the theatre of agonies playing
out in ritual hurt and holy dying,
contest of sacraments in the deep wood;
warrior and warrior-saint pursued
their separate glories in this clearing.

For the absent victors, pelt and powder
were the sanctity of Georgian Bay
and no ritual lingered among trees;
whoever died might yet be called martyr
for what that was worth at bourse or quaie,
far from the land they knew as vacancies.

II

Was it athleticism in dying,
the runner outrunning his nature's pain,
exercise of mastery and disdain
for flesh that hung estranged and burning?
No one goes from the self in suffering,
for torture stops time, this now again
and again, no movement that might sustain
the mind with a heaven of its ending.

Pain for pain, one place became another,
and the Calvary of their devotion
was an agony elsewhere yet the same,
their heart's gaze fixed upon Christ their brother,
who inhabited their silent passion
and the body of that moment in flame.

CARMINE STARNINO
Deaths of the Saints

St. Lucy, flame-proof, needed a firmly speared throat.
St. Christina's was a long job with a pair of pincers.
St. Hippolytus pitied his persecutors who faced him

blood-bespattered, breathing heavily, at wits' end
– he instructed them to bind each arm and leg to a horse
and was torn apart when all four galloped in different directions.

Those strangled, those scourged, those sawn in two.
Limbs flayed to bone. Heads that took hours to lop.
Some thrown to the lions, others drowned with rocks.

St. Simeon who begged for a stake through the heart,
said *thank you* when, heels on his chest, they thrust it deep.
And lucky St. Fergus who passed away in his sleep.

Wayne Clifford
Jane Relents

I knew the city's seventh age.
No one was taken in by Helen.
The Greeks called our Prince Paris felon
to justify their plunder-rage.
Oh, history bleeds its cruelest page
through all the book for us to dwell on.

Then give the consorts each her ease.
They put their backs so in their work.
And tell the princes, cross their knees.
They'll meet none else who'll give a fuck
that old whores go down on their luck
and *heirs apparents* fondle geeze.

Yes, I was there to dry the hands
and hear the crowd shout *"Barabbas!"*
I saw what each prince understands:
The moment one must meet demands,
besides the covering of ass,
puts one the center. Let it pass.

And draw the spikes out one by one.
Stick no more boys up in that tree.
The old man only had one son.
Now pull him down and set him free.
Hold your breath and count to three.

See?
    You're alive.
               The good guys won.

BRIAN BARTLETT
A Skater Tale

      1

A blind man in despair walked with his dog.
Not even sherry like a swallowed flame,
a many-rivered sonata, or his braille
Bulfinch's Mythology cheered him any more.

From a snowy footbridge a whispery rhythm
slowly grew closer, sharper, a skater circling
a small canal. On the island in the oval
the blind man felt no red-cheeked Mercury darting down
his body's frozen streams,

its winged feet snarls of bone and dust
under the raised script's hard snows.

      2

What wild whim did he give in to, following
his dog up the steps of Apollo Sports
where a girl with a peach-soft voice
searched for skates his size? At his back
he sensed skis awaiting fields and woods,
toboggans that had never touched a hill.

Over thick socks, the good fit of new skates
startled him. Flight soared to his mind, promising paths
that start at the feet and stretch away, no horizon
waiting to knock him flat, endless space ahead.

3

At mid-day the mid-city rink lay silent.
He halted, he wavered, he saw himself
a button-eyed scarecrow blown off its perch –
but soon his shoulders and legs recalled it all,
his humming muscles retrieved their buried speeds.
Flying   hawk-sure   exultant –

When a fissure tripped him, he staggered
backwards, keeping his head high. Fallen,
he was a spinning X, his bruised elbow a small price.

His dog licked his face with its hot tongue.
It was the sun grown fleshly, telling him
the cradle of old myths swung in his gasping breath.
In his ears, other children of Mercury gathered.

JAMES REANEY
Don Quixot de la Verismo

Once, *auf Kanada,* I met
A different kind of Don Quixot.
Instead of collecting romances,
He owned several hundreds of realistic novels!
Many copies of James T. Farrell,
And many many copies of Theodore Dreis-
er, illustrated, non-illustrated,
All bought with zeal never sated.
As for Émile Zola – ooh lala, Zoo la la –
His collected works piled on a sofa!

Now this Don Quixot went on a quest
To find nothing of particular interest,
But just to let the environment
Over him be absolutely dominant.
He tried hard not to have adventures,
And talked to people mostly of their dentures.
Until he saw one day
Beside his highway
Giants lined up on the hills.
He thought they were windmills!
And would they grind some flour for him
And fill his water pail to the brim?
Oh, these giants with their giantesses
Of windmills were quite the antitheses.
When he climbed up to them with pail and bag of wheat
Hoping to get something to drink and eat
These giants with terrific ease
Tore him to pieces!
Oh tale of woe!

Another victim of *verismo!*
Don't forget he had a Sancho Panza
Who lagged behind him like a second stanza
And kept telling him they weren't windmills,
"We live in a fairy tale, not in 'real-life' novels!
The Brothers Grimm are right
Dreiser, Farrell and Zola ain't!"
Don Quixot's squire scampered off with a wail,
But not without the wheat and the pail,
Deserting this highway for a nearby wood
As fast as he could!

Norm Sibum
Embarkation of the Argonauts

You put out the word and they come,
  The heroes, as it were, the legends,
So many sons of Poseidon and Zeus –
  They come, fate worn lightly.

And the ship, an entity now, completed,
  By way of roller and hawser and sweat,
Is guided, is coaxed to the sea from the beach,
  Is anchored, marvellous craft,

While the naysayers moan and cry,
  Anticipating the grievous losses,
While the requisite gods, Apollo especially,
  Are propitiated, offered their beef

From stone fat-drenched. While the poet plucks his instrument
  So as to calm debate, smooth over rivalries, bad blood,
So as, perhaps, to wonder
  If he still has it in him

To cause the groves to dance, to alter
  The flight of birds, the stars coming on.
Wine is poured on the roofs of the eager, the arrogant,
  The defiant tongues, and sleep comes.

– Dawn, and it begins, and you go,
  The ship, dream on water, cutting through foam,
You apprehensive, without a plan,
  you and your fools and the unknown.

M. Travis Lane
Gold Fleece

Golden fleece, where are you then, golden fleece?
    Mandelstam, *Collected Poems,* no. 92 (Tr. W.S. Merwin and Olga Carlisle)

From what dark-eyed and heavy-slumbered sleep
might such an apricotted wool
be sheared, washed of its fragrant oils,
and carded in white afternoons
among the rustling lemon trees?

A granite herd
stockades the pasture of my themes
from which each labour doing is undone,
stubborn against my handling.
This is no wall or country that I weave
but a plain language you can't read
unless you bruise your knuckles.

Lazy ones, cover your eyes with sugar sand
and croon an easy poetry
against the on-returning of the sea.
Against these tides my rocks stand firm
and my red beacon.
Sailors, this is home.
    Gold fleece, where are you then, gold fleece?

IV. The Passing and Afterlife of the Gods

P. K. PAGE
The Gold Sun

Trace the gold sun about the whitened sky
Without evasion by a single metaphor.
Look at it in its essential barrenness
And say this, this is the centre that I seek.
  "Credences of Summer," Wallace Stevens

Sky whitened by a snow on which no swan
is visible, and no least feather falling
could possibly or impossibly be seen,
sky whitened like the blank page of a book,
no letters forming into words unless
written in paleness – a pallidity
faint as the little rising moons on nails –
and so, forgettable and so, forgot.
Blue eyes dark as lapis lazuli
trace the gold sun about the whitened sky.

You'll see the thing itself no matter what.
Though it may blind you, what else will suffice?
To smoke a glass or use a periscope
will give you other than the very thing,
or more, or elements too various.
So let the fabulous photographer
catch Phaeton in his lens and think he is
the thing itself, not knowing all the else
he is become. But you will see it clear
without evasion by a single metaphor.

How strip the sun of all comparisons?
That spinning coin – moving, yet at rest
in its outflinging course across the great
parabola of space – is Phoebus,
sovereign: heroic principle,
the heat and light of us. And gold – no less
a metaphor than sun – is not the least
less multiple and married. Therefore how
rid the gold sun of all its otherness?
Look at it in its essential barrenness.

Make a prime number of it, pure, and know
it indivisible and hold it so
in the white sky behind your lapis eyes.
Push aside everything that isn't sun
the way a sculptor works his stone,
the way a mystic masters the mystique
of making more by focusing on one
until at length, all images are gone
except the sun, the thing itself, deific,
and say this, this is the centre that I seek.

E.J. Pratt
Myth and Fact

We used to wake our children when they screamed;
We felt no fever, found no pain,
And casually we told them that they dreamed
And settled them in sleep again.

So easy was it thus to exorcise
The midnight fears the morning after.
We sought to prove they could not literalize
Jack, though the giant shook with laughter.

We showed them pictures in a book and smiled
At red-shawled wolves and chasing bruins –
Was not the race just an incarnate child
That sat at wells and haunted ruins?

We had outgrown the dreams, outrung the knells
Through voodoo, amulet and prayer,
But knew that daylight fastened on us spells
More fearful than Medusa's hair.

We saw the bat-companioned dead arise
From shafts and pipes, and nose like beagles
The spoors of outlaw quarry in the skies
Whose speed and spread made fools of eagles.

We shut our eyes and plugged our ears, though sound
And sight were our front-line defences,
The mind came with its folly to confound
The crystal logic of the senses.

Then turned we to the story-books again
To see that Cyclopean stare.
'Twas out of focus for the beast was slain
While we were on our knees in prayer.

Who were those giants in their climbing strength?
No reason bade us calibrate
These flying lizards in their scaly length
Or plumb a mesozoic hate.

The leaves released a genie to unbind
Our feet along a pilgrimage:
The make-believe had furnished to the mind
Asylum in the foliage.

Draw down the blinds and lock the doors tonight:
We would be safe from that which hovers
Above the eaves. God send us no more light
Than falls between our picture covers.

For what the monsters of the long-ago
Had done were nursery peccadilloes
To what those solar hounds in tally-ho
Could do when once they sniffed the pillows.

W.W.E. Ross
Delphic Apollo

Delphic A-
pollo is
gone from the
haunts that were
sacred in ancient

days in the
morning of
Greece when
light was
supreme.

Can we
discover
here in this
wild clear
rocky region

of the great
foretelling
God some
strong eman-
ation?

KERRY-LEE POWELL
The Answers

Tell the king, the fair-wrought house has fallen. No shelter has Apollo, nor sacred laurel leaves; the fountains now are silent; the voice is stilled.
　　Last prophecy of the Oracle at Delphi

Athens vanishes in a blast of dust. I spent my last night
there with an ex-marine, crowned king of the Phoenix
monster truck circuit, both of us drunk and seeking
oblivion, because the Parthenon was closed for repairs
and the streets stank of garbage and death.
There are whole suburbs in Florida
choked with mournful beauty, their abandoned pools
filling slowly with rain. The Greek hills are strewn
with the half-built villas of luck's has-beens,
their poured foundations at a distance
indistinguishable from ancient ruins. My Phoenix
king's snake-handling Baptist forefathers
have blessed him with vacant eyes and a mistrust
of philosophy. But he knows trauma, blunt
or otherwise, has no beginning, no end,
only knots and kinks around which the mind
bends and groans, the remembered explosions
blooming beneath closed eyes again and again.
From our bus the Aegean is a mass of gleams,
the bleached walls in the villages
blank as the pages of an unwritten book.
We're a time machine, a dented silver capsule
speeding up Mount Parnassus to the Delphic
Oracle with a tour guide in epaulets and fake military
regalia. Bruised, crosshatched with scars,
my Arizonan twitches at each thrust of the bus's engine

then slips back into fitful sleep. He has come to Greece,
like me, to find an explanation for his own heroics,
the way an abandoned child might seek a father
among the relics and unearthed torsos,
but has found so far only sunstroke and Retsina.
I can feel them as we walk the path from parking lot
to ruins: the questions, spoken or etched
on tablets, crushed underfoot like mollusk shells
into fine dust over the millennia.
Our guide tells us about Delphi's glories,
Plutarch's treatise on rust and how through
the mouth of a writhing woman, the Oracle spoke
to anyone who climbed the temple steps with wrung hands,
in tongues and grandiose language,
in beauty and anger and unbearable tenderness,
whose eyes turned inward and tunnelled down the wartorn,
blood-soaked centuries, past the blooming of countless
explosions, to see us staring back, indifferent as ghosts
on the steps to the crumbling stadium, the guide pausing
by an empty pedestal where Apollo's
statue once stood, the passengers disappearing
with cameras over the rock face, snapping fragments
of a moment that they may or may not linger over in years
to come, recalling the smell of pines and diesel,
the silver capsule speeding its way back
to Athens, through groves and along the coast,
and the answers, glancing off rooftops,
striking the cliff face, abrading the rocks.

WARREN HEITI
Sonnets to Orpheus 1.3

She goes to the oracle, she goes inside the temple of stone where everything has stopped, except the ants panicking across the oracle's face, the face pale and hard from the waters of the Hebros, the mouth open, the lips cracked. She stands before the oracle and sings a prayer, and as she sings she watches his closed eyes, his open mouth. She sings a prayer, she asks for water and the oracle does not answer. She sees where the blood has stopped in his throat. She sees where the wind has died into his lips and mouth, where wind has become stone, where stone holds the breath of water and wind is a song that no wind is singing, and she stops her prayer. The ants go across the oracle's lips, they go inside his mouth, they come out of his mouth. She swallows, and watches the ants, and knows they mean nothing. They go across his lips, they go inside his mouth, they come out of his mouth.

She knows he would not ask for tears, she knows he does not need them, she knows the ants mean nothing and knows her tears mean nothing here. The salt in her throat. And she cannot stop. She cannot get the song out of her body. The ants go across the oracle's lips, they go inside his mouth. She touches the oracle's lips with her lips, and goes out of the temple.

ANNE WILKINSON
Twilight of the Gods

One man prayed
"Hold your nuclear Sun
On the Right hand of heaven,"
Another cried,
"The God of Power belongs
On the Left hand with the chosen."

As was to be expected
Neither received a reply.
But how could they admit?
Forging God's signature
Each sat down
And composed a holy writ.

The two books were so similar
They might have been written by brothers;
For absolution both proposed
Last rites, flood-lit.

Robyn Sarah
A Confused Heart

All right, I admit it, I'm to blame,
it's on account of me
the Messiah doesn't come;

I am the blip on the screen,
the cold spot, the dark area you see
with indefinite borders, moving sluggishly

crabwise, with a density all its own,
unabsorbed, indissoluble; the clot
in the body politic – that's me,

accountable by myself (though not alone)
for the tarrying footfall, for our
continuing bad name:

because of my imperfect faith,
my ritual omissions, my mistakes in form,
my little games of nor-care-I,

because I am stiff-necked, and push
the quarrel with God one step too far,
preferring to do the thing my way

rather than not at all (unable
to play by the rules to save my life,
unwilling to drop the ball) –

because I confuse having a part
with holding apart, and star with shield;
because I will always pause

in my studies along the road, to say
How fair is that field,
how fine is that tree;

because I have made strange fire
again and again, and lived,
and the earth has not swallowed me.

A.F. Moritz
To the Still Unborn

You don't know me but I was once watching films and films
of yet another man-caused horror germinating in the depths.
I was sitting alone with a television's loud images of fear,
repetitious and badly made. I was wondering why
I couldn't turn them off. Always an outpost, a small
and stupid crew in some corner of sea floor, void, or desert,
was being assaulted by a beast that enters the human body
and turns it first to a monster bubbling in pain,
then finally to a blank, viscid, and implacable enemy:
image of the human self-experiment. Or rather, this image
as it appears to the hucksters who made these awful movies
and sold them to my nights, otherwise quiet in the hum
of refrigerator engine and whistle of aural nerves decaying.
I wondered why I didn't turn them off and think of you,
didn't pierce through fear of the great strain it would be
to compose my mind's noise, my senses' palsy
the way hands can be folded or legs formed into a root,
the sort of root a canoe's hull or the belly of a tern
offers to water, moving on its own pressure and soft shadow.
Was I hopeless because you were never thinking of me?
But you didn't yet exist then, when I was sitting in my kitchen,
hoping soon to turn off the companionable horror of my day
and think of you, quiet, powerful, come from the future
rescuing me not as I imagined you but as you will be.

Eric Ormsby
Jaham's Poetic Manifesto

"To make the ear
of the *khinzîr*
(that grotty pig!)
lustrous
as the Pleiades ..."

Jaham pondered this and said:
Rather, to make the ears
of the Pleiades
pig-like, that is, porous, gristle-
webbed, conical, tendril-

attuned to the earth.

JOHN THOMPSON
[Ghazal XXI]

I know how small a poem can be:
the point on a fish hook;

women have one word or too many:
I watch the wind;

I'd like a kestrel's eye and know
how to hang on one thread of sky;

the sun burns up my book:
it must be all lies;

I'd rather be quiet, let the sun
and the animals do their work:

I might watch, might turn my back,
be a done beer can shining stupidly.

Let it be: the honed barb drowsing in iron water
will raise the great fish I'll ride

(dream upon dream, still the sun warms my ink
and the flies buzzing to life in my window)

to that heaven (absurd) sharp fish hook,
small poem, small offering.

JAMES POLLOCK
Sailing to Babylon

I sailed a boat to Babylon
and rowed back lonely in the rain.
I struck out down a country lane,
I set my course for Avalon,

but once I'd crossed the Acheron
and slept beside the silver Seine,
I sailed my boat to Babylon
and rowed back lonely in the rain.

I've worshipped at the Parthenon,
I've loved the girls of Aquitaine,
but when they lay my bones in Spain,
O tell the Tetragrammaton
I sailed my boat to Babylon
and rowed back lonely in the rain.

Richard Outram
Ms Cassie Abandoned

The ageless golden wallow
of summer used to be
voluptuous and fruitless.
Between you and me,

most oracles and elders
are too set in their ways,
just can't hack it, not these
indeterminate days.

Look – it's a fine kettle
of harriers; circling they rise
into the all-devouring sun.
The black surprise

is like the stoop of darkness
from some unspoken ring
upon the other of its kind –
the one sure thing.

Beside myself I augur
death's evidence because
it is almost Immortal.
Or once it was.

Jay Macpherson
The Love-Song of Jenny Lear

Come along, my old king of the sea,
Don't look so pathetic at me:
We're off for a walk
And a horrid long talk
By the beautiful banks of the sea.

I'm not Arnold's Margaret, the pearl
That gleamed and was lost in a whirl,
Who simpered in churches
And left him on porches,
But more of a hell of a girl.

Poor old fish, you're no walker at all,
Can't you spank up that elderly crawl?
I'll teach you to hurdle,
Led on by my girdle,
With whalebone, elastic and all.

We'll romp by the seashore, and when
You've enough, shut your eyes and count ten.
I'll crunch down your bones,
Guts marrow and stones,
Then raise you up dancing again.

Some Notes on Context

[Unknown], by Harry Thurston, is the untitled first poem in the collection *Ova Aves* (2011), a series of poems by Thurston paired with Thaddeus Holownia's photographs of bird eggs in the collection of the biology department at Mount Allison University. The egg that inspired the opening poem is "unknown," insofar as the species of bird that laid it is unidentified.

"Our Child Which Art in Heaven," by Gwendolyn MacEwen, is from the opening section of her sequence *The T.E. Lawrence Poems* (1982). "The figure of Lawrence has always fascinated me," MacEwen said: "Lawrence was drawn to the desert Arabs, the Bedouin, among other things by the fact that they felt such great joy in renouncing the pleasures of the world. It was almost a voluptuousness in not having anything, not owning anything, and their relationship to their god was a passionate one. Lawrence was consciously in awe of this, could never achieve it himself, and I feel the same way" (quoted in *Gwendolyn MacEwen, Volume Two: The Later Years,* ed. Rosemary Sullivan).

"The Bible, Notes On," by Souvankham Thammavongsa, is from *Found* (2007), Thammavongsa's second trade-published collection; in her preface to the book she writes: "In 1978, my parents lived in building #48. Nong Khai, Thailand, a Lao refugee camp. My father kept a scrapbook filled with doodles, addresses, postage stamps, maps, measurements. He threw it out and when he did, I took it and found this." Elsewhere, she tells us that the scrapbook is written in Laotian, a language she can speak but cannot read or write ("My Father's Scrapbook," *The New Quarterly* 105).

"PS: Book of Eve" is the third of three "Eve" poems in Beverley Bie Brahic's *White Sheets* (2012). Serving – with its postscript title – as a coda to the collection, it positions Eve as a summative figure for Brahic, a sort of sultry genesiac persona, mother and teacher, in pursuit of the seductive.

The excerpt from ***Ursa Major*** by Robert Bringhurst has its origins in a text spoken by the character of Arcturus in Bringhurst's "polyphonic masque for speakers and dancers," first performed in Regina in March, 2002. The script – really a score, showing multiple parts, including this monologue, overlaid on one another – was published by Gaspereau Press in 2003.

"Fates Worse Than Death," by Don McKay, is the second section of the sequence *Matériel*, which first appeared in McKay's 1997 collection *Apparatus;* it was re-collected in his 2001 prose-book *Vis à Vis.* An earlier vignette in that book defines the sequence title: "In its limited sense matériel is military equipment; in a slightly larger sense it is any equipment owned by an institution. But I'm taking the term to apply even more widely to any instance of second-order appropriation, where the first appropriation is the making of tool[s], or the address to things in the mode of utility .... To make tools into matériel, we engage in a further appropriation. This second appropriation of matter may be the colonization of its death, as in the case of the [displayed, murdered] raven, the nuclear test site, the corpse hung on a gibbet or public crucifixion. On the other hand, matérielization could be a denial of death altogether, as in the case of things made permanent and denied access to decomposition, their return to elements...." The version of the poem printed here is from McKay's *Camber: Selected Poems, 1983-2000.*

The excerpt from Ricardo Sternberg's 1996 book ***Map of Dreams*** is the untitled second poem in the book's second section. The book recounts, in a sequence of lyrics, a story of a quest for various Wandering Islands, one of them, perhaps, the island of poetry.

"Jane Relents," by Wayne Clifford, comes near the end of Clifford's 2009 sequence *Jane Again,* a tribute to and a channelling of Yeats's Crazy Jane – who was herself, it seems, a tribute to and a channelling of a woman named Cracked Mary. Clifford writes: "Cracked Mary might translate today into 'street person', one of the homeless that the system has dispossessed. Yeats offered no explanation for Crazy Jane's craziness, so I've spent decades imagining what might have given her the sauce to answer the bishop" as she does in Yeats's great poem on the subject. Clifford quotes the poem in full, ending with Jane's famous words:

> "A woman can be proud and stiff
> When on love intent;
> But Love has pitched his mansion in
> The place of excrement;
> For nothing can be sole or whole
> That has not been rent."

"Sonnets to Orpheus 1.3," by Warren Heiti, is from *The Metamorphosis of Agriope,* the third section of Heiti's book *Hydrologos* (2011). Agriope is "Another, older name for Eurydike," Heiti tells us. Sonnet 1.3 of Rilke's *Sonnets to Orpheus* ends like this:

Youth, this is not it, your loving, even
if then your voice thrusts your mouth open, – learn

to forget your sudden song. That will run out.
Real singing is a different breath.
A breath for nothing. A wafting in the god. A wind.

(Trans. M.D. Herter Norton)

"**Jaham's Poetic Manifesto**," by Eric Ormsby, is the inaugural poem in *Araby* (2001), in the words of the cover copy "a collection of poems on the adventures, dreams, hopes, and imaginings of two singular characters: Jaham, the 'Father of Clouds,' a semi-nomadic poet and auto-mechanic, and his inseparable sidekick Bald Adham, also a virtuoso mechanic as well as a pillar of Muslim piety ...."

[Ghazal XXI], by John Thompson, is from the ghazal-sequence *Stilt Jack* (1978): a Ulyssean quest-narrative, a love story, a night-sea-journey (these characterizations are Peter Sanger's, from his 2013 entry on Thompson in the on-line *New Brunswick Literary Encyclopedia*) set in rural New Brunswick and, like much myth poetry, at the same time everywhere.

"**Ms Cassie Abandoned**," by Richard Outram, is from Outram's poetic sequence *Ms Cassie*, a collaboration with his wife, the artist Barbara Howard, which was designed and broadcast piecemeal as a series of broadsides under Outram's and Howard's private press imprint, the Gauntlet Press. In 2000, Outram wrote an introduction to the sequence and he and Howard collected the broadsides under a single cover. The sequence has never been published commercially, but is available through the Gauntlet Press exhibition of the Digital Archives Initiative, Memorial University (collections.mun.ca/gauntletpress). The sequence's protagonist, Ms Cassie, is a Cassandra figure transposed into the late 20th century; she is at the same time a figure for what Sanger has called (describing Outram) "a poet armed and a poet prepared to prophesy."

Rosemary Kilbourn is one of Canada's great mythopoeic artists. The wood engraving that is the source of our cover image (***Untitled** [10.3 cm x 13 cm]*) had its origins in a commission that the United Church gave to Kilbourn and to Gwendolyn MacEwen, sometime in the 1960s, to produce image and word, respectively, for the Church's Christmas card. Kilbourn remembers that MacEwen's poem was on the theme of the journey of the magi; this particular engraving went with a section of the poem about "'the sound of wings' as they [the magi] came close to their destination." The engraving is reproduced in Kilbourn's book *Out of the Wood* (Porcupine's Quill, 2012).

Acknowledgements

We would like to thank the authors, publishers, and executors who have granted us permission to republish the poems collected here. We are also grateful to Brian Bartlett, John Barton, Darren Bifford, Stephanie Bolster, Robert Bringhurst, Anne Compton, Melissa Dalgleish, Sandra Djwa, Anita Lahey, Diana Macpherson, Zailig Pollock, and Carmine Starnino, all of whom talked myth-poetry with us, shared the names of possible poets, and/or helped us with permissions inquiries, while this anthology was under construction. Finally, we are grateful to our families, without whom this work could never have been undertaken, much less completed.

Margaret Avison: "Birth Day" from *The Collected Poems of Margaret Avison*, Vol. 1 (Porcupine's Quill, 2003). Copyright © the Estate of Margaret Avison, included by permission of the publisher and the estate. Alfred Bailey: "Gluskap's Daughter" from *Miramichi Lightning: The Collected Poems of Alfred Bailey* (Fiddlehead Poetry Books, 1981). Copyright © the Estate of Alfred Bailey. Brian Bartlett: "A Skater Tale" was published in *Wanting the Day: Selected Poems* © 2003 by Brian Bartlett. Reprinted by permission of Goose Lane Editions. Darren Bifford: "Wedding in Fire Country" from *Wedding in Fire Country* (Nightwood Editions, 2012). Copyright © Darren Bifford, included by permission of the author and the press. Beverley Bie Brahic: "PS: Book of Eve" from *White Sheets* (Fitzhenry & Whiteside, 2012). Copyright © Beverley Bie Brahic, included by permission of the author. Diana Brebner: "Frozen" from *The Ishtar Gate* (McGill-Queen's University Press, 2004). Copyright © the Estate of Diana Brebner, included by permission of the estate. Robert Bringhurst: Excerpt from *Ursa Major* (Gaspereau Press, 2003). Copyright © Robert Bringhurst, included by permission of the publisher and the author. Mark Callanan: "The Myth of Orpheus" from *Gift Horse* by Mark Callanan is used by permission of Signal Editions/Véhicule Press and the author. Wayne Clifford: "Jane Relents," from *Jane Again* (Biblioasis, 2009). Copyright © Wayne Clifford, included by permission of the publisher and the author. Leonard Cohen: "Song." Excerpted from *Let Us Compare Mythologies* by Leonard Cohen. Copyright © 1969 Leonard Cohen. Reprinted by permission of McClelland & Stewart, a division of Penguin Random House Canada Limited, a Penguin Random House

Company. Anne Compton: "Birdlore" from *Asking Questions Indoors and Out* (Fitzhenry & Whiteside, 2009). Copyright © Anne Compton, included by permission of the author. Michael Crummey: "Odysseus as a Boy" is taken from *Under the Keel*, copyright © 2013 by Michael Crummey. Reproduced with permission from House of Anansi Press. www.houseofanansi.com. Mary Dalton: "Salt Mounds, St. John's Harbour" from *Red Ledger* by Mary Dalton is used by permission of Signal Editions/Véhicule Press and the author. Jeffery Donaldson: "Troy" from *Slack Action: Poems* (Porcupine's Quill, 2013). Copyright © Jeffery Donaldson, included by permission of the publisher and the author. Robert Gibbs: "Depth of Field" from *The Essential Robert Gibbs*, ed. Brian Bartlett (Porcupine's Quill, 2012). Copyright © Robert Gibbs, included by permission of the publisher and the author. Richard Greene: "St. Ignace" from *Boxing the Compass* by Richard Greene is used by permission of Signal Editions/Véhicule Press and the author. Steven Heighton: "Were You to Die" is taken from *The Ecstasy of Skeptics*, copyright © 1994 by Steven Heighton. Reproduced with permission from House of Anansi Press. www.houseofanansi.com. Warren Heiti: "Sonnets to Orpheus 1.3" from *Hydrologos* (Pedlar Press, 2011). Copyright © Warren Heiti, included by permission of the publisher and the author. Daryl Hine: "Patroclus Putting on the Armour of Achilles" from *Recollected Poems: 1952-2004* (Fitzhenry & Whiteside, 2007). Copyright © the Estate of Daryl Hine, included by permission of the estate. George Johnston: "Creation" from *Endeared by Dark: The Collected Poems* (Porcupine's Quill, 1990). Copyright © the Estate of George Johnston, included by permission of the estate. Marius Kociejowski: "Coast" from *So Dance the Lords of Language: Poems, 1975-2001* (Porcupine's Quill, 2003). Copyright © Marius Kociejowski, included by permission of the publisher and the author. M. Travis Lane: "Gold Fleece" from *Keeping Afloat* (Guernica, 2001). Copyright © M. Travis Lane, included by permission of the publisher. Douglas LePan: "River-God" from *Weathering It: Complete Poems 1948-1987* (McClelland & Stewart, 1987). Copyright © Don LePan, included by permission of the estate of Douglas LePan. Gwendolyn MacEwen: "Our Child Which Art in Heaven" comes from *The Selected Gwendolyn MacEwen*, published by Exile Editions, Toronto, 2007. Permission for use has been provided by the author's family. Jay Macpherson: "The Marriage of Earth and Heaven" and "The Love-Song of Jenny Lear" from *Poems Twice Told* (Oxford University Press, 1981). Copyright © the Estate of Jay Macpherson, included by permission of the estate. Don McKay: "Fates Worse than Death." Excerpted from *Camber: Selected Poems, 1983-2000* by Don McKay. Copyright © 2004 Don McKay. Reprinted by permission of McClelland & Stewart, a division of Penguin Random House Canada Limited, a Penguin Random House Company. A.F. Moritz: "To the Still Unborn" is taken from *The Sentinel*, copyright © 2008 by A.F. Moritz. Reproduced with permission from House of Anansi Press. www. houseofanansi.com. Daniel David Moses: "Crow Out Early" from *The White Line*

(Fifth House, 1990). Copyright © Daniel David Moses, included by permission of the author. Eric Ormsby: "Jaham's Poetic Manifesto" from *Araby* by Eric Ormsby is used by permission of Signal Editions/Véhicule Press. Richard Outram: "Ms Cassie Abandoned" from *Ms Cassie* (Gauntlet Press, 2000). Copyright © the Literary Estate of Richard Outram, included by permission of the estate. P.K. Page: "The Gold Sun" from *Kaleidoscope: Selected Poems,* ed. Zailig Pollock (Porcupine's Quill, 2010). Copyright © the Estate of P.K. Page, included by permission of the publisher and the estate. Elise Partridge: "Sisyphus: the Sequel" is taken from *Chameleon Hours*, copyright © 2008 by Elise Partridge. Reproduced with permission from House of Anansi Press. www.houseofanansi.com. James Pollock: "Sailing to Babylon" from *Sailing to Babylon* (Able Muse Press, 2012). Copyright © James Pollock, included by permission of the author. Kerry-Lee Powell: "The Answers" from *Inheritance* (Biblioasis, 2014). Copyright © Kerry-Lee Powell, included by permission of the publisher and the author. E.J. Pratt: "Myth and Fact" from *E.J. Pratt: Complete Poems, Part One,* ed. Sandra Djwa and R.G. Moyles. Copyright © University of Toronto Press, 1989. Reprinted with permission of the publisher. James Reaney: *"Don Quixot de la Verismo"* from *Souwesto Home* (Brick Books, 2005). Copyright © the Estate of James Reaney, included by permission of the publisher and the estate. W.W.E. Ross: "Delphic Apollo" from *Shapes and Sounds* (Longman's, 1968). Copyright © the Estate of W.W.E. Ross, included by permission of the estate. Peter Sanger: "After Monteverdi" from *Aiken Drum* (Gaspereau Press, 2006). Copyright © Peter Sanger, included by permission of the publisher and the author. Robyn Sarah, "A Confused Heart" from *A Day's Grace: Poems 1997-2002* (Porcupine's Quill, 2003). Copyright © Robyn Sarah, included by permission of the publisher and the author. Norm Sibum: "Embarkation of the Argonauts" from *Smoke and Lilacs* (Carcanet, 2009). Copyright © Norm Sibum, included by permission of the author. Sue Sinclair: "Orpheus Meets Eurydice in the Underworld" was originally published in *The Drunken Lovely Bird* © 2004 by Sue Sinclair. Reprinted by permission of Goose Lane Editions. Carmine Starnino: "Deaths of the Saints" from *This Way Out* (Gaspereau Press, 2009). Copyright © Carmine Starnino, included by permission of the publisher and the author. Ricardo Sternberg: Excerpt ("No sooner had we left ...") from *Map of Dreams* by Ricardo Sternberg is used by permission of Signal Editions/Véhicule Press and the author. Bruce Taylor: "Orphée" from *No End in Strangeness: New and Selected Poems* (Cormorant Books, 2011). Copyright © 2011 Bruce Taylor, used with the permission of the publisher. John Terpstra: "Genesis" from *Brilliant Falls* (Gaspereau Press, 2013). Copyright © John Terpstra, included by permission of the publisher and the author. Souvankham Thammavongsa: "The Bible, Notes On" from *Found* (Pedlar Press, 2007). Copyright © Souvankham Thammavongsa, included by permission of the publisher and the author. John Thompson: "[Ghazal XXI]" is taken from *Stilt Jack*, copyright © 1978 by John Thompson.

Reproduced with permission from House of Anansi Press. www.houseofanansi.com. Harry Thurston: "[Unknown]" from *Ova Aves* (Anchorage Press, 2011). Copyright © Harry Thurston, included by permission of the publisher and the author. Anne Wilkinson: "Twilight of the Gods" from *Heresies: The Complete Poems of Anne Wilkinson 1924-1961* by Anne Wilkinson is used by permission of Signal Editions/Véhicule Press.

Every effort has been made to trace copyright holders. The editors and publisher apologize if any material has been included without appropriate acknowledgement, and would be glad to correct any errors, in future editions.